Anton's

Publishing

Primer

How to publish your first book

Anton's Fast Track
Publishing Primer

Anton's

Publishing

Primer

How to publish your first book

By Anton Anderssen

Hartforth Publications

4177 Garrick Ave   Warren Michigan 48091
(586) 757 4177 Voice (313) 557 6367 Fax
International Standard Book Number:
0 9666119 93
Printed in the United States
First Edition. Second Printing.
Library of Congress Control Number:
2002108784

Dedication

To Marilyn Mach vos Savant
who inspired me to keep my dream
alive that one day my books would be
published.

Anton Anderssen

CONTENTS.

About the Author.. 7
Acknowledgements.. 8
Forward... 9
Setting up a publishing house................................ 11
ISBN...17
Bar Codes..18
Preparing your manuscript.....................................21
LCCN...26
Printing..29
Covers...37
Custom Cover Design Companies...........................38
Copyright...40
Reviews...41
Books in Print..47
Distributors...48
Vanity Publishing..52
Promoting your book..53
Further reading...54
Special offers..55

About the Author

Dr. Anton Anderssen earned a Juris Doctor degree from Wayne State University School of Law, and

continued with coursework in Labor Law. He is a member of Mensa, the high IQ society, and several other high IQ groups including Triple 9 Society, ISPE, & Prometheus. He is a PADI certified open water scuba diver, has NASA moon rock certification, has studied 27 different languages, performs piano during the holiday season at venues such as the Detroit Institute of Arts, is legally titled in Great Britain as "The Lord of Hartforth," works as a producer for the TV Show "Perspective on the Arts," develops adult enrichment classes for 20 public school districts and community colleges, has been a volunteer at Gilda's Club, The International Institute, American Red Cross, and Public Television, and has written several books and training manuals.

Acknowledgments

I am grateful to Dr. Raymond Archer of Indiana University who taught me how to love books. He also taught me how to think, and how to experience life. He taught me French language and grammar. He taught my Freshman English class, and inspired me to write. He taught my comparative literature classes and introduced me to the world's greatest literature, the arts, and their inter-relationship. I owe my happiness to Professor Archer...he taught me how to find meaning in my life.

Forward

Anyone can write a book. Anyone can become a publisher. The publisher is the one who owns the ISBN number, puts up the money to print the book, and markets the book. This book is for people who just want to get their books published without going through a lot of headaches or mortgaging their houses. As a matter of fact, this book is for people who want to spend under $777 to turn their dreams of publishing a book into a reality through self-publishing.

This book is not about how to get someone else to do your work. It is not about how to get someone else to publish you. This is for the "Do It Yourself" kinds of people who want to separate the nuts and bolts from the fluff. This book will teach you the basic information you will need to get your books printed and available to the public at a very low cost.

Everyone has a book inside him waiting to be written. Everyone has something to tell the world, as a result of the experiences that occur in life. Everyone has something to say. Life has a way of providing interesting stories to us without much dredging. Think about all those skeletons in your closet, wouldn't they make a juicy book? Now is the time to say it.

When all is said and done, and you are lying in your grave, what will you have left behind to keep your memory alive? Will your experiences, thoughts, knowledge, wisdom, values, and beliefs die with you, or will you make sure a part of you lives on through your book?

There are lots of books on the market that teach you how to publish books. That's fine if you have the time to read 500 pages and learn everything there is to know about publishing. Some of us just want the bottom line. This book has just the facts. It is a practical publishing primer to put you on the fast track to becoming a published author. It is not meant to be a complete reference - just the key information.

Setting up yourself as a publishing house

The first step in becoming a publisher is announce to the world you are a publishing house. This is very easy to do. In most states you visit the county clerk and fill out a form called "Conducting Business Under an Assumed Name" or DBA (Doing Business As) form. You pay a nominal fee, like $10 to file the papers, then like magic, you are a publishing house.

This serves as a license to conduct business. This is not the same thing as filing articles of incorporation, which can be a lengthy process. The DBA is a fast-track way to becoming a self-publisher. Incorporating will cause you income tax headaches, filing grief, lots of record keeping, and double taxation. When you choose the fast track DBA method, you cannot call yourself Inc., Limited, etc., and you cannot be a partnership. You must be a sole proprietorship to stay on the fast-track method.

Business Registration Certificate
Person Conducting Business
Under Assumed Name or Partnership
County of   Office of County Clerk
Filing Fee

D.B.A. File No. _____
Certificate exp _____
Certificate Filed _____
Dissolved _____

THE UNDERSIGNED hereby certifies, under the provisions of P.A. No. 101, P.A. of Mich., for the year 1907, as amended, that the following person (or persons) now owns, carries on, conducts or transacts, or intends to carry on, conduct, or transact, a business, or maintain an office or place of business, in the County of _____ State of Michigan, under the name, designation or style set forth below:

1. NAME OF BUSINESS _____

2. STREET ADDRESS OF BUSINESS _____

   CITY _____ STATE _____ Zip _____

3. BUSINESS mentioned above (Insert "IS" or "IS NOT") _____ a partnership. If a partnership, complete sections 4,5, and 7. If not a partnership, complete sections 4,5, and 6.

4. NAME OF PERSON OR PERSONS, owning, transacting, or composing the above business, and the home address of each.

Name	House Number/Street (No P.O. Boxes)	City/State/Zip Code
(Print)		
(Print)		
(Print)		
(Print)		

5. SIGNATURES OF ALL PERSONS LISTED ABOVE (Acknowledged before a Notary Public)

   (Signature) _____
   (Signature) _____
   (Signature) _____
   (Signature) _____

6. STATE OF MICHIGAN Subscribed and Sworn to before me this _____ day of _____ A.D., _____
   COUNTY OF
   (Signature) _____
   (Print) _____
   Notary Public, _____ County, Michigan
   My Commission expires: _____

7. PARTNERSHIP CERTIFICATE. The undersigned hereby certify under the provisions of P.A. No. 164, P.A. of Mich., for the year 1913, as amended, that the business named herein is a partnership.

STATE OF MICHIGAN
COUNTY OF   I, _____

one of the co-partners of the said firm _____
(Write in name of firm on this line)
do hereby certify that all co-partners of said firm have herein above individually subscribed their respective names as witnessed by myself, and that the place of residence of each said co-partner as above written is true and correct.

(Signed) X _____
(ONE OF THE CO-PARTNERS OF ABOVE NAMED FIRM)

STATE OF MICHIGAN Subscribed and Sworn to before me this _____ day of _____ A.D. _____
COUNTY OF
(Signature) _____
(Print) _____
Notary Public, _____ County, Michigan
My Commission expires: _____

(Form below for use of County Clerk)

STATE OF MICHIGAN
COUNTY OF   I, _____ Clerk of the County of _____ and the Circuit Court thereof, do hereby certify that I have compared the foregoing copy of Business Registration Certificate with the original of record in my office, and that the same is a correct transcript therefrom, and of the whole of such original.
In Testimony Whereof, I have hereunto set my hand and affixed the

seal of said Circuit Court, this _____ day of
_____ , A.D., _____ .

By: _____
County Clerk/Register of Deeds

By: _____
Deputy Clerk

NOTE: This Certificate must be renewed within (5) years from date. If you change your place of business you must notify this office. If you change the personnel listed above on an assumed name, you must file Notice of Dissolution. or file an amended Partnership Certificate with this office.

"Person" means one or more individual, partnerships, trusts, fiduciaries, or other entities capable of contracting except corporations and limited partnerships. MCLA 445. 1 AS AMENDED 1980.

Once you have your DBA / business license, you need a sales tax number. Whenever you sell your books to consumers inside your state, you have to collect your state sales tax, then send the tax on to your state's Department of Treasury. Since the number of books you will be selling at first will probably be a humble amount, you will not likely be required to file sales tax reports very often with your state. Commonly, you need only remit the sales taxes once per year. Even then, the first 10 dollars or so per month of sales tax collected may be exempt from remittance to your state. You will not be collecting sales tax if you send your books out of state, or if you are selling to a tax-exempt entity like a church or school.

When filling out the sales tax form, be certain to let your state know you are small potatoes! Keep yourself out of hot water - don't try to boast grand sales predictions, because they'll just hound you or audit you for the money they think you are collecting.

Michigan Department of Treasury and Un-employment Agency
515 (Rev. 6-98). Formerly C-3400.

REGISTRATION FOR   **TAXES**

1. Federal Employer Identification Number (Required for UA)
If you do not have an FEIN, call the IRS at 1-800-829-1040.
1a. UA No.

2. Complete Company Name or Owner's Full Name (include, if applicable, Corp., Inc., P.C., L.C., L.L.C., L.L.P., etc.)

3. Business Name, Assumed Name or DBA (as registered with the county)

Legal Address	4A. This address is for all legal contacts. Enter number and street (no P.O. boxes).	Business Telephone
	City, State, ZIP	County
Mailing Address	4B. This address is where all tax forms will be sent unless otherwise instructed.	If this address is for an accountant, bookkeeper or other representative, attach a Power of Attorney.
	City, State, ZIP	
Physical Address	4C. This address is the actual location of the business in Michigan. Enter number and street (cannot be a P.O. box number).	
	City, State, ZIP	County

5. Type of Business Ownership (check one only)

☐ (1) Individual (Sole Proprietorship)
☐ (2) Husband/Wife
☐ (3) Partnership
     ☐ (3) Registered Partnership, Agreement Date:_____
     ☐ (3) Limited Partnership - Identify all general partners below
☐ (34) Limited Liability Co. or Partnership
     ☐ Domestic (Mich)
     ☐ Professional
     ☐ Foreign (Non-Mich)

☐ (4) Michigan Corporation
     ☐ (1) Subchapter S
     ☐ (2) Professional
☐ (5) Non-Mich. Corporation
     ☐ (1) Subchapter S

☐ (6) Trust or Estate (Fiduciary)
☐ (7) Joint Stock Club or Investment Co
☐ (8) Social Club or Fraternal Org.
☐ (9) Other (Explain)

Date of Incorporation			State of Incorporation	Michigan Department of Consumer & Industry Services Identification No.
Mo.	Day	Year		

6. Which taxes do you expect to owe?   What date will that liability begin?   How much of each tax do you estimate you will owe each month?

	Mo. Day Year	Up to $65	Up to $300	Over $300
☐ Sales Tax		☐ Up to $65	☐ Up to $300	☐ Over $300
☐ Use Tax		☐ Up to $65	☐ Up to $300	☐ Over $300
☐ Income Tax Withholding		☐ Up to $65	☐ Up to $300	☐ Over $300
☐ Single Business Tax		How many people will you employ who are subject to Michigan withholding? _____		
☐ Motor Fuel Taxes_____	Treasury will review your registration and send you any necessary tax application forms.			
☐ Tobacco Products Tax_____	Treasury will review your registration and send you any necessary tax application forms.			
☐ UA Unemployment Tax	Attach Schedules A, B (if successor) and C. Enclose a copy of your Articles of Incorporation or Organization.			

7. Estimated annual Michigan gross receipts?   **GROSS RECEIPTS** are from (a) sales of inventory items, (b) rental or leases, (c) performance of
☐ Up to $250,000   ☐ Over $250,000   services, interest, royalties, etc., to the extent they are derived from business activity.

Complete all information for each owner, partner, member or corporate officer. Attach a separate list if necessary.		
8A. Name (Last, First, Middle. Jr./Sr./III)	Social Security Number	
Title	Date of Birth	
Residence Address (Number, Street)	Driver License/Michigan Identification	
City, State, ZIP	Home Telephone	
8B. Name (Last, First, Middle, Jr./Sr./III)	Social Security Number	
Title	Date of Birth	
Residence Address (Number, Street)	Driver License/Michigan Identification	
City, State, ZIP	Home Telephone	

PLEASE DETACH BEFORE MAILING.

After you fill out the registration for taxes form, you will receive a tax ID. This is for sales tax, not to be confused with an EIN (which is a federal ID you must have whenever you have employees). Since your book printing orders are in humble numbers, there should be no need for employees.

At the end of the tax year, you will need to file a Schedule C : Profit or Loss from a Business and Schedule SE : Self Employment taxes.

SCHEDULE C (Form 1040)	**Profit or Loss From Business** (Sole Proprietorship)	OMB No. 1545-0074
Department of the Treasury Internal Revenue Service (99)	▶ Partnerships, joint ventures, etc., must file Form 1065 or Form 1065-B. ▶ Attach to Form 1040 or Form 1041. ▶ See Instructions for Schedule C (Form 1040).	Attachment Sequence No. 09

Name of proprietor		Social security number (SSN)	
A Principal business or profession, including product or service (see page C-1 of the instructions)		**B** Enter code from pages C-7 & 8	
C Business name. If no separate business name, leave blank		**D** Employer ID number (EIN), if any	

E Business address (including suite or room no.) ▶
City, town or post office, state, and ZIP code

F Accounting method: (1) ☐ Cash (2) ☐ Accrual (3) ☐ Other (specify) ▶

G Did you "materially participate" in the operation of this business during 2000? If "No," see page C-2 for limit on losses . . . . ☐ Yes ☐ No

H If you started or acquired this business during 2000, check here . . . . ▶ ☐

Part I Income

1 Gross receipts or sales. **Caution.** If this income was reported to you on Form W-2 and the "Statutory employee" box on that form was checked, see page C-2 and check here . . . . . ▶ ☐	**1**	
2 Returns and allowances	**2**	
3 Subtract line 2 from line 1	**3**	
4 Cost of goods sold (from line 42 on page 2)	**4**	
5 Gross profit. Subtract line 4 from line 3	**5**	
6 Other income, including Federal and state gasoline or fuel tax credit or refund (see page C-2)	**6**	
7 Gross income. Add lines 5 and 6 . . . . ▶	**7**	

Part II Expenses. Enter expenses for business use of your home only on line 30.

8 Advertising	**8**		**19** Pension and profit-sharing plans	**19**	
9 Bad debts from sales or services (see page C-3) . . .	**9**		**20** Rent or lease (see page C-4):		
10 Car and truck expenses (see page C-3) . . .	**10**		**a** Vehicles, machinery, and equipment .	**20a**	
11 Commissions and fees .	**11**		**b** Other business property . .	**20b**	
12 Depletion . . .	**12**		**21** Repairs and maintenance . .	**21**	
13 Depreciation and section 179 expense deduction (not included in Part III) (see page C-3) . .	**13**		**22** Supplies (not included in Part III) .	**22**	
14 Employee benefit programs (other than on line 19) . .	**14**		**23** Taxes and licenses	**23**	
15 Insurance (other than health) .	**15**		**24** Travel, meals, and entertainment:		
16 Interest:			**a** Travel	**24a**	
a Mortgage (paid to banks, etc.)	**16a**		**b** Meals and entertainment		
b Other	**16b**		**c** Enter nondeductible amount included on line 24b (see page C-5) .		
17 Legal and professional services . . .	**17**		**d** Subtract line 24c from line 24b	**24d**	
18 Office expense . . .	**18**		**25** Utilities	**25**	
			26 Wages (less employment credits) .	**26**	
			27 Other expenses (from line 48 on page 2)	**27**	

28 Total expenses before expenses for business use of home. Add lines 8 through 27 in columns . . . ▶	**28**	
29 Tentative profit (loss). Subtract line 28 from line 7	**29**	
30 Expenses for business use of your home. Attach Form 8829	**30**	
31 Net profit or (loss). Subtract line 30 from line 29. • If a profit, enter on **Form 1040, line 12,** and also on **Schedule SE, line 2** (statutory employees, see page C-5). Estates and trusts, enter on Form 1041, line 3. • If a loss, you **must** go to line 32.	**31**	

32 If you have a loss, check the box that describes your investment in this activity (see page C-5).
• If you checked 32a, enter the loss on **Form 1040, line 12,** and also on **Schedule SE, line 2** (statutory employees, see page C-5). Estates and trusts, enter on Form 1041, line 3.
• If you checked 32b, you **must** attach Form 6198.
  32a ☐ All investment is at risk.
  32b ☐ Some investment is not at risk.

For Paperwork Reduction Act Notice, see Form 1040 instructions. Cat. No. 11334P Schedule C (Form 1040) 2000

Be certain you take advantage of all the tax write-offs available to you as a publishing house – the writers' conferences, cost of books, etc. There's no reason to over-pay Uncle Sam!

Take all available business write offs

As long as you created your business as a DBA, your business taxes will simply be part of your personal business taxes. This fast-track strategy will greatly reduce your headaches!

Apply for your ISBN numbers

Whoever owns the ISBN number, owns the rights to publish the book. If you borrow an ISBN number from someone, money from the sales of that book will go to him, because he is technically the publisher. The only true way to be a self publisher is to own all of your ISBN numbers.

Every time you create an edition of a book, it needs a new ISBN number. A new edition means that the book has changed in content. If you order 100 books from a printer, then order 100 more, you are not creating a new edition unless the content has changed. Your first book is marked "First Edition."

The U.S. ISBN Agency is responsible for the assignment of the ISBN Publisher Prefix to those publishers with a residence or office in the U.S. and are publishing their titles within the U.S.

U.S. ISBN Agency
630 Central Avenue
New Providence, NJ 07974
Tel: 877-310-7333   908-665-6770
888-269-5372   Fax: 908-665-2895
isbn-san@bowker.com
www.isbn.org   www.bowker.com
http://www.isbn.org/standards/home/isbn/us/application.asp

You will register your publishing house with the ISBN, and then receive an allotment of numbers which you will assign to each of your book titles. This program is administered by RR Bowker www.bowker.com/ There is a fee charged for the numbers, however it is important that YOU own the ISBN numbers to retain control over your books.

Getting Your Bar Code

Once you have your ISBN number, you can order a bar code. The type of bar codes that publishers use is called the Bookland EAN bar code, and it is not the same thing as the UPC code on merchandise. The only thing that a book bar code says is the ISBN number and the price of the book. Every time you change the price of your book, you have to get a new bar code. Sometimes the printer will create a bar code for you and print it onto the back cover of your book. Other times you will need to buy some bar code stickers and place them there by hand.

BAR CODE GRAPHICS, INC.
875 N. Michigan Ave, Ste. 2640
Chicago, IL 60611
Tel: 312-664-0700
800-662-0701
Fax: 312-664-4939
EMAIL: sales@barcode-us.com
WEB: www.barcode-us.com

THE BARCODE SOFTWARE CENTER
1113 Hull Terrace
Evanston, IL 60202
Tel: 847-866-7940
800-229-5794
Fax: 847-866-9836
EMAIL: sales@makebarcode.com
WEB: www.makebarcode.com

FOTEL, INC.
41 West Home Ave
Villa Park, IL 60181
Tel: 630-834-4920
800-834-4920
Fax: 630-834-5250
EMAIL: coding@fotel.com
WEB: www.fotel.com

BAR CODE GRAPHICS
375 Fifth St
Columbus, OH 43219
Tel: 800-932-7801
Fax: 312-664-2291
EMAIL: sales@barcode-us.com
WEB: www.barcode-graphics.com

FILM MASTERS
11680 Hawke Rd.
Columbia Station, OH 44028
Tel: 440-748-8060
800-541-5102
Fax: 440-748-2258
EMAIL: barcodes@en.com
WEB: www.filmmasters.com

PARAGON DATA SYSTEMIZES, INC.
2218 Superior Ave.
Cleveland, OH 44114
Tel: 216-621-7571
800-211-0768
Fax: 216-621-2651
EMAIL: info@paragondatasystems.com
WEB: www.paragondatasystems.com

Bar Code
is read
by scanner

The Bookland EAN Bar Code is placed on the back of the book. It contains the ISBN and price of the book in computer-readable format. It is not the same thing as a UPC (Uniform Pricing Council) bar code which identifies the manufacturer of particular merchandise.

Preparing your manuscript

There are several ways to prepare your manuscript for the printer. The fast-track method is to simply print to your printer's server from your word processing software on your PC. This can be done fast track if you print your book through Instant Publisher http://www.instantpublisher.com/default.asp?afcc=1099

Instant Publisher is cheap, fast, and provides great quality for the price. Instant Publisher uses Print on Demand technology, as opposed to offset printing. For huge orders like 5,000 copies, you are better off using an offset printer. For printing your first book, you are better off using print on demand because you can order as few as 25 books.

The best value for your dollar is to use a standard trim size. Those sizes are 4 1/4 inches by 7 inches, 5 1/2 inches by 8 1/2 inches, 8 1/2 inches by 11 1/2 inches, and 6 inches by 9 inches. The best value in the standard trim sizes is the 5 1/2 inches by 8 1/2 inches (like this book). This size also works best for consumers because it easily fits into a purse or briefcase.

If you are using Microsoft Word as your text editor, click on File, then Page Setup. Set your margins to: Top 1", Bottom 3", Left 2.3", Right 2.3", Gutter 0", Header 0.5", Footer 2". Select gutter TOP. That will make your pages look like the pages in this book. When you are ready for page numbers, click Insert, Page Numbers. Set numbers for "Top of Page" and "Center" to look like this book.

Font size should be from 11 to 13 points. Select a font style that compliments your subject matter. The font style in this book is called Comic Sans MS. It resembles elementary school writing, and suggests simplicity, no-nonsense style, uncomplicated communication, and personal approach. Comic Sans was never meant to be used as a type font for rapid reading. If you are writing a huge novel for people who read quickly, you should use Times Roman as your font. Use Comic Sans MS when you want to present your

information in the most uncomplicated, unpretentious, straight-forward manner.

When you insert clipart into MS Word text, double click on it (if it is in color) and change the "image control" color to grayscale (not black and white). If you want to print in color, you are better off to do a book entirely in color, and take advantage of full-color books, which are more expensive than the black and white books as exampled in this book. This company also does POD (Print on Demand) full color:

www.instantpublisher.com/default.asp?afcc=1099

Instant Publisher lets you include as many black and white images / photos as you want. Some printers charge fees as much as $15 per image, because they have to do extra scans. Some printers will let you laser print (not ink jet) your pages and send the laser originals to them as camera ready art. Other printers will require you to flow your word processing text into Quark Xpress or PageMaker format and send it to them on a CD. Unfortunately, Quark Xpress and PageMaker are not cheap, and most people don't know how to use them. Fast track publishers will find Instant Publisher to be the most practical method for printing books.

Book on CD Rom

www.instantpublisher.com/default.asp?afcc=1099

If you choose offset printing (the opposite of print on demand) you will need to keep in mind some very important considerations to keep your price down: Keep your page numbers in multiples of 16 or 32. Stick to black plus 1 more color on your cover if you are doing offset. Order at least 2500 copies of your book when using an offset printer, otherwise POD is going to be cheaper. For offset paper, ask for house stock 60 pound white or 50 pound white (thinner), or ask them what they use as house stock.

Do not use offset printing unless you order at least 2500 copies, because that's where the price breaks come in. Most people just starting out will avoid offset printing.

It's probably a good idea to stay away from

ordering huge quantities of your book until you know you can sell it easily, and you know all the errors have been corrected. Most people will print 100 to 500 copies at a time using POD (Print on Demand) because they constantly are making revisions to the book, and don't want to be saddled down with 10,000 copies of a book that has errors or out of date information. The key is to be practical and reasonable.

Unfortunately, the reality in the book world is that only a small percentage of books (regardless how they are published) actually make money. Before you begin your book project, be certain you understand that this may be a labor of love.

Dr. Anton Anderssen, author, with
Marvin Hamlisch. Marvin wrote dozens of
successful Broadway musicals, hit songs, and
soundtracks. He is Barbra Streisand's orchestra
conductor, and is the conductor for the National
Pops Symphony. He is well known for writing the
hit "The Way We Were" sung by Barbra Streisand.

Getting your Library of Congress Number

A Library of Congress control number is a unique identification number that the Library of Congress assigns to the records created for each book in its cataloged collections. Librarians use it to access the associated bibliographic record in the Library of Congress's database, and if you want to sell your books to libraries, you must obtain this number. The Library of Congress assigns this number while the

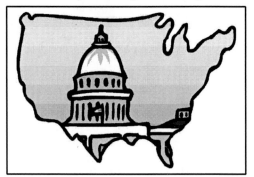

book is being cataloged. A control number can be assigned before the book is published through the Pre-assigned Control Number Program. You print this number on your copyright page of your book. Register at http://pcn.loc.gov/pcn/ You must send a copy of your book to the Library of Congress after you get your printed copies. Send them to:

Library of Congress Cataloging in Publication Division
101 Independence Ave., S.E.,
Washington, D.C. 20540-4320

1. Go to the EPCN homepage: http://pcn.loc.gov/pcn

2. Click the "Account Number" button.

3.   Enter your account number and password in lower case with no spaces. If this is the first time you access the EPCN program, you are required to change your password and confirm the change. This is done by entering the new password in the "New Password" space and re-entering it in the "Confirm New Password" space. Your new password cannot exceed a total of eight letters   and/or numbers. Click the "Sign On" button.

4.   When you enter the system, you will be provided three options:

"PCN Application"
Click this option to request a Preassigned Control Number.

"PCN Change Request"
Click this option to report a change to a title for which a Preassigned Control Number has already been assigned.

"Publisher Information Change Request"
Click this option to update or change information provided when you first applied to participate in the PCN program.

For security reasons, if you access the system and leave it unattended for an extended period of time, the system will time out and you will have to reenter your account number and password. These features require that your browser will accept cookies. For Internet Explorer, click on Tools, click the Internet Options in the drop-down menu, click the Security tab, click the Custom Level button, and click on the enable cookies buttons and click on Reset. For Netscape, click on Edit, click the Preferences in the drop-down menu, click Advanced, click on accept cookies button and click OK.

Once you have published three books, you are eligible to participate in the CIP program and receive library-cataloguing data for printing on your copyright page. The Cataloging in Publication Office supplies postpaid mailing labels once you have been admitted to the CIP program.

Printing your book

You will want to send for price quotes from many companies if you want offset printing, because the price could vary from 3,000 to 40,000 dollars. For most first time book publishers, you will print a more humble amount of books, and therefore use POD (Print on Demand) technology, such as is offered by Instant Publisher. Print on Demand can have your books in your hand within 10 days. Offset printing could take several months. Print on Demand is the most practical for most people, because you can order a small number of books and can use easy text editing programs such as Microsoft Word.

For POD, the most practical fast track printer is Instant Publisher. See
http://www.instantpublisher.com/default.asp?afcc=1099

For over 2500 copies, please contact a printer and get a price quote for your book project.

Overseas Printing Corp.
99 The Embarcadero
San Francisco, CA 94105
Tel: 415-835-9999
Fax: 415-835-9899
Email: hal@overseasprinting.com
Web: www.overseasprinting.com

Palace Press International
1299 4th St., Ste.305
San Rafael, CA 94901
Tel: 415-455-2480

Fax: 415-455-2490
Email: gordon@palacepress.com
Web: www.palacepress.com

Marrakech Express Printing Inc.
720 Wesley Ave.
Tarpon Springs, FL 34689
Tel: 727-942-2218
      800-940-6566
Fax: 727-937-4758
Email: print@marrak.com
Web: www.marrak.com

Rose Printing Company
2503 Jackson Bluff Road
Tallahassee, FL 32304
Tel: 850-576-4151
Fax: 850-576-4153
Email: charlesr@roseprinting.com
Web: www.roseprinting.com

Whitehall Printing Company
4244 Corporate Square
Naples, FL 34104
Tel: 941-643-6464
      800-321-9290
Fax: 941-643-6439
Email: info@whitehallprinting.com
Web: www.whitehallprinting.com

D.B. Hess Company
1530 McConnell Road

Woodstock, IL 60098
Tel: 815-338-6900
Fax: 815-338-9608
Web: www.dbhess.com

Evangel Press
P.O. Box 189
Nappanee, IN 46550
Tel: 800-253-9315
Fax: 574-773-5934
Email: glenwyn@evangelpress.com
Web: www.evangelpress.com

Prinit Press
211 N.W. 7th St.
Richmond, IN 47374
Tel: 765-966-7130
Fax: 765-966-7131
Email: michael@prinitpress.com
Web: www.prinitpress.com

Phoenix Color Corp.
540 Western Maryland Parkway
Hagerstown, MD 21740
Tel: 301-733-0018
Fax: 301-791-9560
Email: khartman@phoenixcolor.com
Web: www.phoenixcolor.com

King Printing Company, Inc.
181 Industrial Ave.
Lowell, MA 01852

Tel: 978-458-2345
Fax: 978-458-3026
Email: chinai@kingprinting.com
Web: www.kingprinting.com

Huron Valley Printing
4557 Washtenaw Ave.
Ann Arbor, MI 48108
Tel: 734-971-1700
Fax: 734-971-6420
Email: sales@hvpi.com
Web: www.hvpi.com

McNaughton & Gunn, Inc.
960 Woodland Dr.
Saline, MI 48176
Tel: 734-429-8712
Fax: 800-677-BOOK
Email: ronm@mcnaughton-gunn.com
Web: www.bookprinters.com

Boyd Printing Company, Inc.
49 Sheridan Ave.
Albany, NY 12210
Tel: 800-877-2693
Fax: 518-436-7433
Email: jcarey@boydprinting.com
Web: www.boydprinting.com

C & C Offset Printing Co., Ltd.
401 Broadway, Ste. 2015
New York, NY 10013-3005

Tel: 212-431-4210
Fax: 212-431-3960
Email: newyorkinfo@ccoffset.com
Web: www.ccoffset.com

Palace Press International
180 Varick St., 10th Fl.
New York, NY 10014
Tel: 212-462-2622
Fax: 212-463-9130
Email: paolo@palacepress.com
Web: www.palacepress.com

BookMasters, Inc.
2541 Ashland Rd.
Mansfield, OH 44905
Tel: 419-589-5100
　　　800-537-6727
Fax: 419-589-4040
Email: info@bookmaster.com
Web: www.bookmasters.com

The C.J. Krehbiel Company
3962 Virginia Ave.
Cincinnati, OH 45227
Tel: 513-271-6035
　　　800-598-7808
Fax: 513-271-6082
Email: rickh@cjkrehbiel.com
Web: www.cjkrehbiel.com

C & C Offset Printing Co., Ltd.

P.O. Box 82037
Portland, OR 97282-0037
Tel: 503-233-1834
Fax: 503-233-7815
Email: cclark@ccoffset.com
Web: www.ccoffset.com

Maverick Publications, Inc.
63324 Nels Anderson Rd.
Bend, OR 97701
Tel: 541-382-6978
Fax: 541-382-4831
Email: gary@mavbooks.com
Web: www.mavbooks.com

The P.A. Hutchison Company
400 Penn Ave.
Mayfield, PA 18433
Tel: 570-876-4560
      800-USA-PRNT
Fax: 570-876-4561
Email: chutchison@pahutch.com
Web: www.pahutch.com

CadmusMack
1991 Northampton St.
Easton, PA 18042
Tel: 610-250-7264
Fax: 610-250-7202
Email: mackj@cadmus.com
Web: www.cadmusmack.com

Starr Toof Book Division
670 S. Cooper St.
Memphis, TN 38104
Tel: 901-274-3632
    800-722-4772
Fax: 901-274-6191
Email: ccoon@starrtoof.com
Web: www.starrtoof.com

Morgan Printing
900 Old Koenig Ln., Ste 135
Austin, TX 78756
Tel: 512-459-5194
Fax: 512-451-0755
Email: books@morganprinting.org
Web: www.morganprinting.org

Leo Paper USA
1180 N.W. Maple St., Ste. 102
Bellevue, WA 98027
Tel: 425-646-8801
Fax: 425-646-8805
Email: peter@pacificpier.com

Banta Book Group
460 Ahnaip St., Curtis Reed Plaza
Menasha, WI 54952
Tel: 920-751-7221
Fax: 920-751-7362
Email: jspringer@banta.com
Web: www.banta.com

University of Toronto Press Incorporated
5201 Dufferin Street, Toronto, Ontario
Canada M3H 5T8
Tel: 416-667-7788
Fax: 416-667-7803
Email: printing@utpress.utoronto.ca
Web: www.utpress.utoronto.ca

Webcom Limited
3480 Pharmacy Ave., Toronto, Ontario
Canada M1W 2S7
Tel: 416-496-1000
Fax: 416-496-1537
Email: webcom@webcomlink.com
Web: www.webcomlink.com

Offset printing is done 16 or 32 pages at a time on a huge sheet of paper

Selecting your book cover

Many printers offer custom work. You pay them by the hour for their art department to create a beautiful cover for your book. This costs about $50 per hour. Most printers offer a limited number of color covers with everything done except writing the title of your book, the author's name, and the bar code. These stock covers are usually the best value, and they also let you create your book fast-track without headaches. You can also send in your camera ready art for the cover and it would be printed in 1 color on your cover. That's probably not a very good idea because it will make your book look cheap.

If you want the title and author name on the spine, the book must contain at least 90 pages. (45 pieces of paper is 90 pages.)

Book Cover Design Companies

Robert Howard Graphic Design, Robert Howard, 631
Mansfield Drive, Fort Collins, CO 80525. Tel: (970)
225-0083; email: rhoward@frii.com.
http://www.BookGraphics.com.

Arrow Graphics, Inc., Alvart Badalian, PO Box 291,
Cambridge, MA 02238.
Tel: (617) 926-8585; Fax: (617) 926-0982; e-mail:
arrow@us1.channel1.com.

Dunn + Associates, Mary Jo Jirik, PO Box 870,
Hayward, WI 54843. Tel: (715) 634-4857; Fax: (715)
634-5617. info@Dunn-Design.com,
http://www.Dunn-Design.com

Lightbourne, Gaelyn Larrick & Shannon Bodie, 258 A
Street, #5, Ashland, OR 97520. Tel: (800) 697-9833;
Tel: 541-488-3060; Fax: (541) 482-1730;
Gaelyn@Lightbourne.com ;
http://www.Lightbourne.com.

Quest Press, Pamela Terry, 1858 So. Crescent Heights
Blvd., Los Angeles, CA 90035. Tel: 323-935-6666;
Fax: 323-934-2881; pam@atwtraveler.com .

Knockout Design, Peri Poloni, 3784 Archwood Road,
Cameron Park, CA 95682.
Tel: 530-676-2744; Fax: 530-676-2741;
peri@KnockOutBooks.com ;
http://www.KnockOutBooks.com.

R.J. Communications, Ron Pramschufer, 51 East 42nd
Street, #1202, New York, NY 10017. Tel: 800-621-
2556; Fax: 212-681-8002; West Coast Office
tel: 800-754-7089; Ron@RJC-LLC.com;
http://BooksJustBooks.com

BookMasters, Inc., Sherry Ringler, 2541 Ashland
Road, Mansfield, OH 44905. Tel: (800) 537-6727;
tel: (419) 589-5100; fax: (419) 589-4040;
info@bookmaster.com; http://www.BookMasters.com.

Be It Now/Karen Ross Design, Karen Ross, 12516
Washington Place, Los Angeles, CA 90066. Tel: 310-
915-0920; Fax: 310-390-0419; Karoons@yahoo.com;
http://www.BeitNow.com/PublishingDesign.htm.

Anton with singer / songwriter Gary Pucket.
Gary is best known for his song "Woman, oh Woman,
have you got cheating on your mind?"

Copyright your book

Copyright protection is secured from the time the work is created in tangible form. The copyright in the work immediately becomes the property of the author who created the work. Only the author can claim copyright. In the case of works made for hire, the employer and not the employee is considered to be the author. A book is automatically protected under copyright laws from the moment of its creation and is ordinarily given a term enduring for the author's life plus an additional 70 years after the author's death.

To register a work, send the following three items in the same envelope or package to:

Library of Congress Copyright Office
101 Independence Avenue, S.E.
Washington, D.C. 20559-6000

- ❖ A properly completed application form TX.
- ❖ A nonrefundable filing fee
  NOTE: Copyright Office fees are subject to change. For current fees, please check the Copyright Office Website at www.loc.gov/copyright, write the Copyright Office, or call (202) 707-3000.
- ❖ A non-returnable deposit: 2 copies of the book being registered.

http://www.loc.gov/copyright/search/cohm.html

Where to Send Your Book for Reviews

American Book Review, Rebecca Kaiser, Illinois State University, Campus Box 4241, Normal, IL 61790; Tel: (309) 438-3026; Fax: (309) 438-3523. This bimonthly, with a circulation of 15,000, reviews 240 books each year.

Baker & Taylor. To establish a business relationship with Baker & Taylor, contact Robin Bright, Publishers Services, PO Box 6885, Bridgewater, NJ 08807; Tel: (908) 218-3803; brightr@btol.com; http://www.btol.com.

Baker & Taylor, Academic Library Services Selection Department, PO Box 6885, Bridgewater, NJ 08807; Tel: (908) 704-1366, for their Current Books for Academic Libraries plan. Enclose a photocopy of the Advanced Book Information (ABI) form. See http://www.btol.com.

Booklist, American Library Association, 50 E. Huron St., Chicago, IL 60611; Tel: (800) 545-2433 or (312) 944-6780; Fax: (312) 440-9374; http://www.ala.org/booklist. You should have sent bound galleys to Booklist some months earlier.

Chicago Tribune Books, Carolyn Alessio, 435 N. Michigan Ave., Chicago, IL 60611 Tel: (312) 222-3232. http://chicagotribune.com/leisure/books/.

Choice, Editorial Dept., 100 Riverview Center, Middletown, CT 06457; Tel: (860) 347-6933; Fax: (860) 704-0465; choicemag@ala-choice.org; www.ala.org/acrl/choice/home.html. Choice is a publication of the Association of College and Research Libraries, a division of the American Library Association. Choice reviews 6,600 books annually for the $300-million academic library market: high school, college and special libraries. Monthly except August. Circulation: 4,800.

Feature News Service, Jim White, PO Box 19852, St. Louis, MO

63144-2096; Tel: (314) 961-9827. Reviews books for 87 weekly papers.

Gale Group, Attn: Contemporary Authors, 27500 Drake Rd., Farmington Hills, MI 48331; Tel: (800) 877-GALE or (248) 699-4253; Fax: (248) 699-8070; alan.hedblad@galegroup.com. Contemporary Authors will not list you in their directory if they think your books are self-published. http://www.galegroup.com.

Horn Book magazine, 56 Roland St. #200, Boston, MA 02129; Tel: (800) 325-1170 or (617) 628-0225; Fax: (617) 628-0882. Horn Book reviews about 420 books each year for children and young adults. It is published bimonthly and has a circulation of 24,000. See http://www.hbook.com.

Hungry Mind Book Review, Bart Schneider, 1648 Grand Ave., St. Paul, MN 55105; Tel: (651) 699-2610; Fax: (651) 699-0970. Hungry Mind Review is a quarterly book review magazine founded in 1986 and distributed free in more than 600 independent bookstores around the country. Each print issue is built around a particular theme and includes reviews and essays by some of America's finest writers. See http://www.bookwire.com/hmr.

H.W. Wilson Co., Attn: Nancy Wong, Cumulative Book Index, 950 University Ave., Bronx, NY 10452; Tel: (800) 367-6770 or (718) 588-8400; Fax: (800) 590-1617 or outside U.S. and Canada, (718) 590-1617; custserv@hwwilson.com; http://www.hwwilson.com. Books must have at least 100 pages and a print run of at least 00 copies.

Independent Publisher magazine, Jenkins Group, 121 E. Front St., #401, Traverse City, MI 49684; Tel: (800) 706-4636 or (231) 933-0445; Fax: (231) 933-0448; jenkinsgroup@publishing.com. Bimonthly, Independent Publisher reviews 75-100 titles every issue. Circulation: 7,000. See http://www.independentpublisher.com/

Ingram Book Company, Express Program, PO Box 3006, La Vergne, TN 37086. The book must not be marked or identified as a promotional copy. Enclose your brochure and discount schedule (a higher discount on single orders will allow them to give stores a discount that will increase sales). See http://www.ingrambookgroup.com/Pub_Info/newpubinfo/.

Kirkus Reviews, 770 Broadway, NYC, NY 10003-9595. Tel: 646-654-4602; fax 646-654-4706; kirkusrev@kirkusreviews.com. You should have sent bound galleys to Kirkus some months earlier.

KLIATT Young Adult Paperback Book Guide, Paula Rohrlick, 33 Bay State Rd., Wellesley, MA 02481; Tel: (781) 237-7577; kliatt@aol.com; http://hometown.aol.com/kliatt. KLIATT annually reviews some 1,600 softcover books for young adults. The magazine is bimonthly and has a circulation of 2,300.

Library Journal, Barbara Hoffert, 245 W. 17th St., New York, NY 10011; Tel: (888) 800-5473 or (212) 463-6818; Fax: (212) 463-6734. Again, you should have sent bound galleys some months earlier. This is a confirmation copy to show the book has been published.

Library of Congress Acquisitions and Processing Division, Washington, DC 20540, along with your brochure and dealer discount schedule. See http://www.loc.gov.

Library of Congress Exchange and Gift Division, Gift Section, Washington, DC 20540. See http://www.loc.gov.

Los Angeles Times Book Review, Steve Wasserman, Times Mirror Square, Los Angeles, CA 90053; Tel: (800) LATIMES or (213) 237-5000; Fax: (213) 237-4712. See http://www.latimes.com.

Midwest Book Review, James A. Cox, 278 Orchard Dr., Oregon, WI 53575; Tel: (608) 835-7937; mwbookrevw@aol.com. Jim favors the small press and will review your book sooner than most reviewers. His reviews are also posted at Amazon.com and other sites. See http://www.execpc.com/~mbr/bookwatch.

Newsday, Estelle Miller, Two Park Ave., New York, NY 10016;
Tel: (212) 251-6623; Fax: (212) 696-0590;
muchnick@newsday.com. Newsday reviews general-interest
books such as fiction, history, politics, biographies and poetry.
They do not review how-to books. Send books to the appropriate
departmental editor. Circulation: 800,000 daily, 950,000 Sunday.
See http://www.newsday.com/nd1/more/books.htm.

New York Review of Books, 1755 Broadway, Floor 5, New York,
NY 10019; Tel: (212) 757-8070; Fax: (212) 333-5374;
nyrev@nybooks.com; http://www.nybooks.com. This biweekly
(except January, July, August and September, when it is monthly)
magazine publishes reviews, prints excerpts and buys serial rights.
They review 400 books each year, and the circulation is 130,000.

New York Times, Daily Book Review Section, 229 W. 43rd St.,
New York, NY 10036; Tel: (212) 556-1234; Fax: (212) 556-7088.
See http://www.nytimes.com/books.

Patrician Productions, Victor Kassery, 145 W. 58th St., New York,
NY 10019; Tel: (212) 265-5612. Some 500 books are reviewed
annually for radio and TV.

Success Stories. Go to http://ParaPublishing.com and click on
Success Stories. Log your book with a description, bibliographic
information, price and source. Interested surfers will come
directly to you. Free. Do not send a book, just log on and register.

Publishers Weekly, Attn: Weekly Record, 360 Park Avenue South,
13th Floor. New York, NY 10010-1710 Tel: 646-746-6400; Fax:
(212) 463-6631. You should have sent bound galleys to PW some
months earlier. This is a confirmation copy to show the book has
been published.

Rainbo Electronic Reviews, Maggie Ramirez, 8 Duran Court,
Pacifica, CA 94044; Tel: (650) 359-0221. Reviews 300 books
annually and publishes them on GEnie online service

Reader's Digest Condensed Books, John Bohane, Editor in Chief,

Pleasantville, NY 10570; Tel: (914) 244-1000; Fax: (914) 238-4559;john.bohane@readersdigest.com; http://www.readersdigest.com.

Reference and Research Book News, Jane Erskine, 5739 NE Sumner St., Portland, OR 97218; Tel: (503) 281-9230; Fax: (503) 287-4485; booknews@booknews.com; http://www.booknews.com. This quarterly, with a circulation of 1,700, reviews some 1,200 books per issue.

Reference Book Review, Cameron Northouse, PO Box 190954, Dallas, TX 75219; Tel: (972) 690-5882. This semiannual has a circulation of 1,000 and reviews some 200 books per year.

Romantic Times, Nancy Collazo, 55 Bergen St., Brooklyn, NY 11201; Tel: (718) 237-1097; Fax: (718) 624-2526; info@romantictimes.com. Rave Reviews folded into Romantic Times, which is a monthly aimed at consumers and focuses on nonfiction best sellers and all genres of fiction except westerns. Over 150 reviews are printed in each edition. See http://www.romantictimes.com.

San Francisco Chronicle, Attn: David Kipen, Book Editor, 901 Mission, San Francisco, CA 94103; Tel: (415) 777-6232; Fax: (415) 957-8737. Circulation: 570,000 daily, 715,000 Sunday. See http://www.sfgate.com/eguide/books/

School Library Journal, Attn: Trevelyn Jones, 245 W. 17th St., New York, NY 10011; Tel: (212) 463-6759; Fax: (212) 463-6689; tjones@cahners.com. This is a confirmation copy to show the book has been published.

Small Press Review, Attn: Len Fulton, PO Box 100, Paradise, CA 95967; Tel: (800) 477-6110 or (530) 877-6110; Fax: (530) 877-0222; dustbooks@dcsi.net; http://www.dustbooks.com. This monthly publication has a circulation of 3,500 and specializes in fiction and poetry.

USA Today, Diedre Donahue, Book Editor, 1000 Wilson Blvd., Arlington, VA 22229; Tel: (703) 276-3400 or (202) 276-6580;

ddonahue@usatoday.com. This daily national newspaper prints reviews every Friday and other times under special subject areas such as sports, money, lifestyle, or art and entertainment. Circulation: 1.9 million. See http://www.usatoday.com/life/enter/books/leb.htm.

Voice Literary Supplement, Village Voice, Joy Press, 36 Cooper Square, New York, NY 10003; Tel: (212) 475-3300; Fax: (212) 475-8944; editor@villagevoice.com. They review 500 books each year in 10 issues. Circulation: 180,000.
See http://www.villagevoice.com/vls.

Washington Post, Marie Arana, Book World, 1150 15th St. NW, Washington, DC 20071; Tel: (202) 334-6000; Fax: (202) 334-5059; aranam@washpost.com. Circulation: 780,000 daily, 1,100,000 Sunday. The Post reviews about 2,000 general fiction and nonfiction books each year. A favorable review in the New YorkTimes or the Washington Post tends to stimulate good reviews in the book sections of smaller newspapers. See http://www.washingtonpost.com/wp-srv/style/

Books in Print

Once ISBNs have been assigned to products they should be reported to R.R. Bowker as the database of record for the ISBN Agency. Companies are eligible for a free listing in various directories such as Books in Print, Words on Cassette, The Software Encyclopedia, Bowker's Complete Video Directory, etc. NOTE: Receiving just your ISBNs does NOT guarantee title listings. To ensure your titles get in the Books in Print database you must submit your title information. Book titles should be registered with Books in Print at www.bowkerlink.com

The BowkerLink system provides publishers with an automated tool to update or add to their listings in Bowker's databases. Publishers may also view and update their publisher contact information. http://www.bowkerlink.com/corrections/bip/ItemEdit .asp

Anton with singer/songwriter BJ Thomas, best known for singing "Raindrops keep falling on my head"

Distribution

Borders , Barnes & Noble , Waldenbooks

Most people sell their books to family and friends. They may give speeches then sell their books from a table at the back of the auditorium. Others sell at conventions, meetings, or simply out of the trunk of their car.

Small bookstores are happy to sell your book on consignment. Just drop by with a few copies and ask them what their procedure is. Once you are listed in Books in Print from Bowker, the bookstores begin ordering from you "special order" whenever a customer asks for your book.

If you do not have a distributor and want to submit your book to Barnes & Noble. Contact them at (732) 656 2000.

Barnes & Noble, Inc.

Booksellers Since 1873
DISTRIBUTION CENTER
100 Middlesex Center, Jamesburg, NJ 08810
Phone (732) 656-2000   Fax (732) 274-9703

HARTFORTH PUBLISHING
Anton Anderssen
4177 Garrick Ave
Warren, MI 48091

Dear Anton:

Thank you for your interest in Barnes & Noble Distribution Center's Extended Title Base Program.

We welcome the opportunity to review your title(s) as a candidate for placement in our Distribution Center. In order to complete this process, we request that you send a sample of your title(s) to the Publisher Services Department for review. If you have multiple titles, please submit samples that best represent your product offering, along with a copy of your most recent catalog. Please mail finished samples to:

Barnes & Noble Distribution Center
Attn: Pamela Day, Publisher Services Department
100 Middlesex Center Boulevard
Jamesburg, New Jersey 08831

Once your title(s) has been reviewed, you will receive notification from me. If it is determined that we are unable to carry your title(s) at this time, we will return the sample(s) to you upon request. Please include this request when submitting your sample(s) to us.

Again, we thank you for your interest in Barnes & Noble Distribution Center's Extended Title Base program and look forward to receiving your sample.

Kindest regards,

Pamela Day
Publisher Services Representative
Barnes & Noble Distribution Center

If you do not have a distributor and want to submit your book to Borders and WaldenBooks, call their New Vendor Acquisitions Line at 734-477-1333 for recorded instructions.

To sell your books through Amazon.com, visit http://amazon.com/advantage/books . You send them a supply of your books and they will do all fulfillment.

To be eligible for Amazon.com Advantage:

- ❖ Each book you wish to enroll must have an ISBN.
- ❖ You must have distribution rights for each title you wish to enroll.
- ❖ You must be located in North America (U.S., Canada, or Mexico).
- ❖ You must have an e-mail address and Web access.
- ❖ Your book must have an ISBN printed on the cover.
- ❖ All books added to your Amazon.com Advantage membership must have a Bookland EAN bar code.

You will apply to have your titles added to Amazon.com's inventory. After you are approved, within 24 hours you will receive another e-mail from Amazon which will include your first Amazon.com Advantage order for these titles. It will also provide instructions for accessing your Advantage account so you can confirm the order online and ship the items requested. You must ship the complete order within 7 days of the e-mail order request.

Next you will add marketing content to your catalog page. Your titles will be greatly enhanced by adding cover art and descriptive information to your catalog pages. You will find all the instructions and many helpful tips at the online Marketing Resource Center. To access this information:
-    Go to http://www.amazon.com/advantage
-    Click the Log In button at the left
-    Enter your account login and password
-    From the Account Maintenance page, click the appropriate Marketing Resource Center link for your books.

If you need to make any corrections to the online catalog pages for your titles, please send your correction to book-typos@amazon.com and be explicit.

If you have further questions, e-mail Amazon at advantage@amazon.com.

Vanity Publishing

Vanity Publishing is when you pay a company from $3,000 to $50,000 to "publish" your manuscript. They

provide an ISBN (maybe the same ISBN is printed in 100 different customers' books), they provide "editing" (they run it through a spell checker), they provide "illustrations" (clip art), and they "promote" (make you buy your book from them for a horrible price). Stay away from Vanity Publishing. See http://www.bbbsouthland.org/ (topics of interest : Vanity Publishing).

Self-Publishing is not the same thing as vanity publishing. Self publishing involves setting yourself up legally as a publishing house, getting all your own ISBN numbers, LCCNs, etc.

Promoting Your Book

https://parapublishing.com/dls/woexyqfp/112SecretLi
st.pdf   This is a free document detailing places to
promote your book.

Online bookstores
http://www.amazon.com
http://www.bn.com
http://www.borders.com
http://www.booksamillion.com/ncom/books?
http://www.seekbooks.com
http://www.elgrande.com
http://www.Ecampus.com

Publishers Directory is a directory in which you may have a free listing. For an application form, contact Gale Group, 27500 Drake Rd., Farmington Hills, MI 48331; Tel: (800) 347-GALE or (248) 699-4253; Fax: (800) 414-5043; http://www.galegroup.com.

Baker & Taylor. To establish a business relationship ith Baker & Taylor, contact Robin Bright, Publishers ervices, PO Box 6885, Bridgewater, NJ 08807; Tel: 908-541-7000; brightr@btol.com www.btol.com

Further Reading

The Self-Publishing Manual : How to Write, Print and Sell Your Own Book by Dan Poynter. Paperback: 432 pages ; Publisher: Para Publishing; ISBN: 1568600739; 13th edition (July 2001)

Writing Nonfiction : Turning Thoughts into Books by Dan Poynter. Paperback: 168 pages ; Publisher: Para Publishing; ISBN: 156860064X; (April 2000)

Make Money Self-Publishing : Learn How from Fourteen Successful Small Publishers by Suzanne P. Thomas. Paperback: 288 pages Publisher: Gemstone House Publishing; ISBN: 0966469127; (September 27, 2000)

http://www2.oakland.edu/contin-ed/writersconf/
The Annual Writers' Conference held on the Oakland University campus in Rochester, Michigan.

http://www.mauiwriters.com/
Maui Writers Conference

http://www.parapub.com Dan Poynter's Self Publishing

Thank you for purchasing a copy of this book. Here's a special offer for promotional copies of <u>Anton's Publishing Primer</u> at a special price to give to your friends.

Send $10 per book, plus $2 flat rate for shipping regardless of the number of copies ordered. On your check's memo area write promotional code "Publish Book Special" and make check payable to Anton Anderssen. You will receive your book from the author's promotional printings, and therefore they could be very slightly different from this book (e.g. no bar code or price printed on the cover, etc.) Stock may be limited. Will ship whenever promotional copies become available. Mail to

Anton Anderssen   4177 Garrick Ave
Warren Mi 48091

Please do not make any shipping inquiries until you are certain your check has cleared your bank.

To join Anton's fan club, and hear about his latest news, see http://groups.yahoo.com/group/Anton

Blue Sky Tours

http://www.BlueSkyTours.com/

Thinking of attending the Maui Writers Conference or going to Hawaii to get inspiration for your book?? Call Blue Sky phone 800 678 2787 or fax 800 747 1221 and tell them you are a student from Anton Anderssen Travel and give them our account number 23 757 417(7). Or log on to the Internet using logon ID anton@antontravel.com password: love4anton   The prices are phenomenal

Carnival Cruise Lines

http://www.bookccl.com/

When calling in as a student travel agency intern, tell them Anton Anderssen Travel's telephone number 586 757 4177, and CLIA number 00 56 1971. Phone Carnival 800 327 9501 or 888 CARNIVAL. If using the internet, go to www.bookccl.com, click on LOGIN and enter ID: student and password: iloveanton   After you log on, you can see all the specials which have been faxed to us at http://www.bookccl.com/salestools/FunFaxes/default.asp Carnival is the world's most popular cruise line. To get brochures, click on the brochures button but use your address in the boxes instead of Anton Anderssen Travel, so it comes to your house. For brochures, you can call Carnival's Inside Sales Team at (800) 327-7276. Carnival fun ship website support desk 800 845 2599 from 9am to 8pm.   To   get   brochures,   just   go   to http://www.bookccl.com/ click on LOGIN, LoginID= student   password= iloveanton   At the scroll down bar which says Sales and Collateral scroll down to Brochure Request. Select 50 Fleet brochures, then click Continue. Type over the info for the address part only.